VOLUME 2

Cut it Out Seattle!

An art book by Rudy Willingham

Published by RudyCorp 2020

Remember when you were a kid, and you'd look up at the sky and say "that cloud looks like a dinosaur"? I do the same thing with my art. I look at my surroundings and try to **re-imagine what the world could be.**

I use paper cutouts as opposed to Photoshop or spray paint because it reminds me of being a little kid (I'm also too old and slow to be running away from the police). It gives my art a human element that often gets lost in today's digital world.

If I want to transform a big object like a building, I hold up cutouts and use forced perspective to create a form of collage art. If the object is smaller, I use tape to create **street art that cheers up my neighbors.** Most people love them, although there are some Karen's out there. To be fair, when I'm scouting locations, measuring things, and taking pictures, it looks like I'm planning a robbery (which is why I take my baby girl with me now).

Don't worry Karen, **I'm just trying to spread a little joy during these hard times.** Look through the book and you'll get it.

- Rudy

Dedicated to my wife Reagan and daughter Lily, our greatest creation ever.

GROUND

U.F.Doh!

Shoutout to the only 90's baseball star

Shot for the

Seattle Sounders

before their 2019 championship match.

SOUTH STAND

WHILE IN PUBLIC
WEAR A MASK
ONE WAY
ONE WAY

I never expected my art to be **hung in so many bathrooms**. I'm honored... I think?

Here you go **bro.**
WORKING HOMEKEEPING
MEA & DEA
ARTIFICIAL COLORS
at least 30% Post-Consumer Plastic.
for The Caldrea Company
Racine, WI 53403 USA
PLASTIC BOTTLE

SEATTLE-07-2
ONE
L VE
SHAUN
FUHR
BLACK FATHERS
MATTER
CAFE

Everyone's hair during
COVID.

The only one excited about

social distancing.

Aesthetic Elmo.

UP is a berry good movie.

(I just became a dad, which means I can use puns with im**pun**ity.)

Hogwarts
SCHOOL
To Ac rict

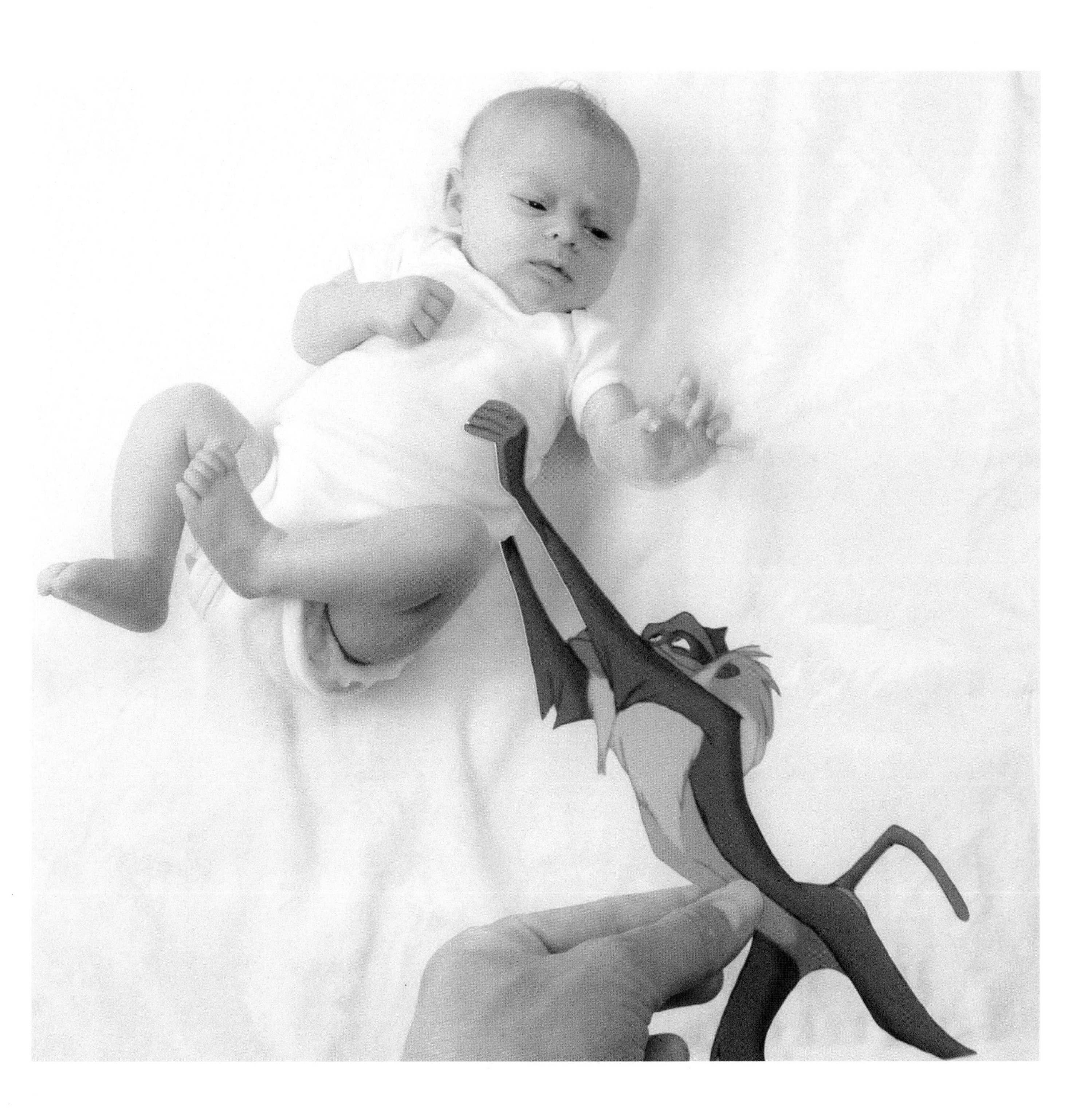

My daughter's birth announcement pics. She's 1-month old and **I'm already embarassing her.**

DJ Lily

My wife when she was a UW Cheerleader.
Go Dawgs!
W

My therapist recommended I maintain a more

positive body image.

Figured out why the

West Seattle Bridge

is closed.

Mood.

The Chihuly exhibit is

so sick.

My favorite
pair of boots.
(shot for Rhein Haus)

Art to promote **Elysian Brewing's** Dayglow IPA.

Shot at **Poquitos** to promote their
Holiday movie nights.

When Marshawn Lynch came back to the Seahawks,

it was a Christmas miracle.

PUBLIC
MARKET
ONE
WAY
Hot Spiced Cider

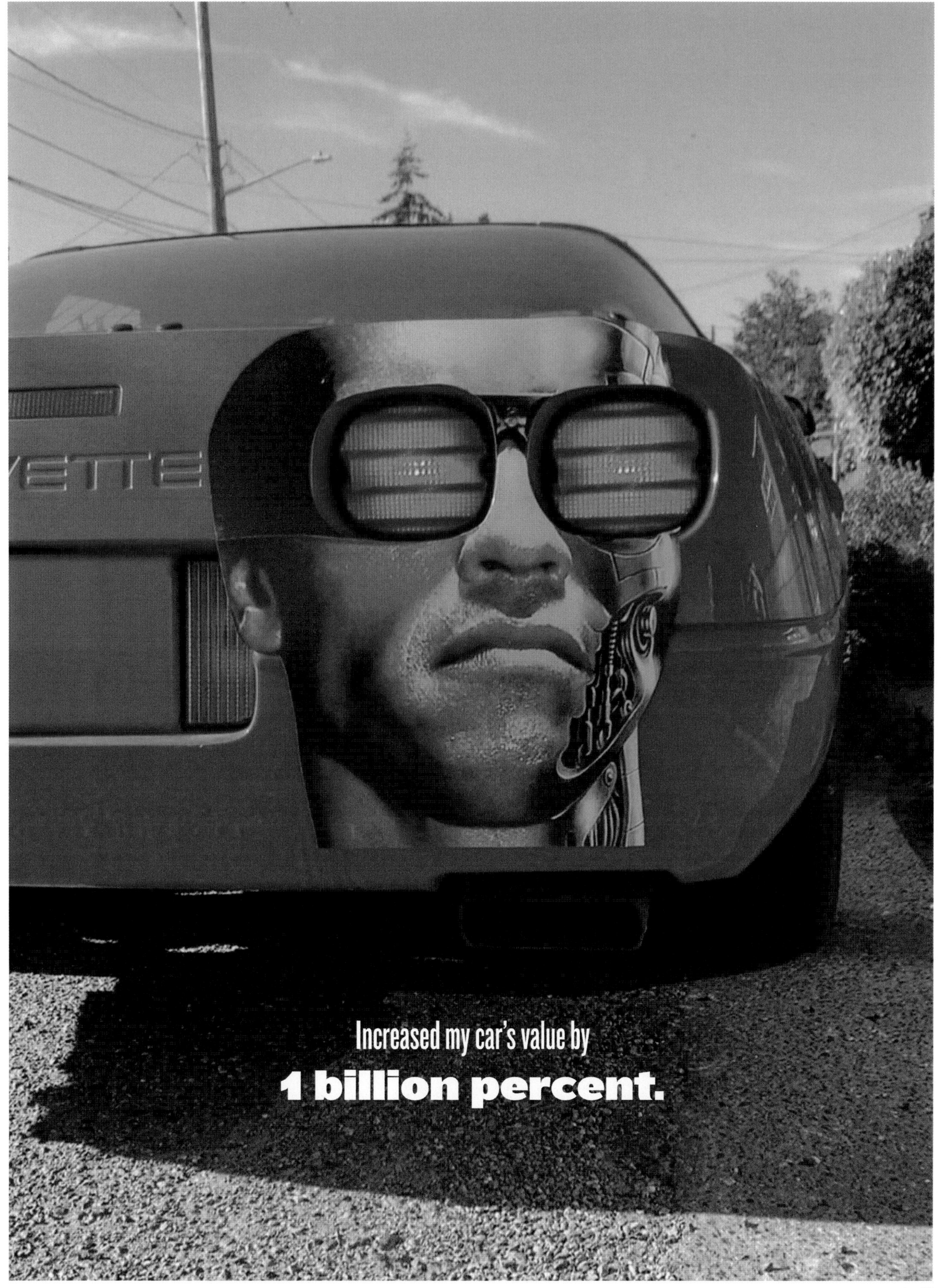
VETTE
Increased my car's value by
1 billion percent.

24 12 FL. OZ. SLIM CANS
BUD LIGHT
100 CALORIES | GLUTEN FREE | 2g CARBS | MADE PURE®
DWIGHT CLAW
HARD SELTZER
BEET
FLAVORED
SPIKED SPARKLING WATER
WITH A HINT OF BEET
100 CALORIES 5% ALC/VOL GLUTEN FREE
6 CANS
CONTAINS ALCOHOL · HARD SELTZER WITH FLAVORS
100 CALORIES | GLUTEN FREE | 2g CARBS | MADE PURE®
WHITE CLAW
HARD SELTZER

Art to promote Elysian Brewing's

Rolling Stone Lager.

RIP

RBG.

RIP

John Lewis.

RIP
George Floyd.

RIP

Breonna Taylor.

Thank you so much for buying this book and taking a **journey through my brain.** I hope you had as much fun looking through it as I did making it.

Made in the USA
Monee, IL
17 December 2020